Little Old Lady Recipes

Little Old Lady Recipes

{ Comfort Food *and* Kitchen Table Wisdom }

by Meg Favreau
Photographs by Michael Reali

QUIRK BOOKS

PHILADELPHIA

Library of Congress Cataloging in Publication Number: 2011922695

ISBN: 978-1-59474-518-8

Printed in China

Typeset in Mrs. Eaves, Sackers Gothic, Bembo, and Nobel

Designed by Katie Hatz
Production management by John J. McGurk
Photographs by Michael Reali

Quirk Books
215 Church Street
Philadelphia, PA 19106
quirkbooks.com

10 9 8 7 6 5 4 3 2 1

....

Disclaimer: Like many little old ladies, we don't worry too much
about precise times or temperatures or expiration dates. We love
leftovers. And we sure don't have weak stomachs. So use your
common sense when you're cooking recipes from this book (or
any other). If you don't like it, don't eat it. And if it smells bad, it's
probably rotten. These are rules that'll serve you well in life and
in the kitchen.

TABLE *of* CONTENTS

WHAT *the* HECK HAPPENED *to* FOOD?

Sure, people are still *eating,* but I'm not sure if I understand what. Protein bars? I'll be darned if I can understand how a foil-wrapped hunk that tastes like a chocolate-dipped cow pie is supposed to replace a meal. Square-inch pieces of fish topped with a single sprout and a hibiscus flower flown in from France? Haute cuisine belongs in some distant future when we're all wearing silver clothing. Green juices? The only place seaweed should be is under my feet once a year when I go to the shore, and even then I can barely stand the stuff, all squishy and smelling like salt water's unwashed underwear.

Food should be food. You shouldn't need to go to the corners of the earth to get it or use some crazy gizmo to prepare it. Life was better when the most confusing thing served was a hot dog—and even then, we understood what went in 'em. We just didn't really want to think about it.

It's time we get back to cooking the comforting foods that made family dinners great. We should be following the advice of the women who made those meals, the women who alternated between doting mothers and tough-as-nails disciplinarians, ladies who worked, raised families, hosted great parties, and made the best out of the worst.

Simple, good, and sassy: little old ladies know how to bring the goods to the kitchen. And it's my hope that with this book, you will, too.

BREAKFASTS *and* COFFEE KLATCH

Some people point to video games or guns or those sneakers with wheels in them to show what's wrong with America. But I say this country went south when TV and magazines started reminding people to eat breakfast, and it was actually news. Darn right, it's the most important meal of the day. Heck, there was a time when we barely had the food to eat breakfast, and now people want to skip it because they need to lounge in bed an extra 20 minutes? Remember this: Early to bed, early to rise makes a man healthy, wealthy, and full of bacon.

APPLESAUCE

2 1/2 lbs cooking apples
1/2 cup sugar
1 tbsp lemon juice

Wash, quarter, and core apples. Add about 1 cup of water to barely cover, cook until nearly soft, and then stir in sugar. Add a pinch or two of nutmeg and cinnamon if you want more flavor. Cook a few minutes longer. Mash. Makes enough to serve with dinner and have leftovers to can or freeze.

Cider Applesauce

Skip the lemon juice, halve the sugar, and replace the water with apple cider.

Canned Applesauce

Boil your jars to make sure they're sterile. Fill them with applesauce and run a knife around the inside to get rid of air bubbles. Put on lids and boil on a canner ring for 20 minutes. If any of the jars don't seal, put them in the fridge and eat them soon. Nobody likes botulism.

BLUEBERRY MUFFINS

1 cup blueberries	1 egg, beaten
2 cups flour	4 tsp baking powder
¼ cup butter	½ tsp salt
¼ cup sugar	1 cup milk

Make a batch of these muffins on Sunday afternoon, and you'll have something to grab any morning of the week that you don't have time for bacon and eggs.

Toss blueberries in ¼ cup of the flour and let them sit an hour.

Cream butter and sugar and beat in the egg. In a separate bowl, mix baking powder and salt into the rest of the flour. Stir flour mixture and milk into the butter mixture. Gently stir in floured berries last. Scoop into buttered muffin tins and bake 25 minutes in a 425°F oven. **Makes 12 muffins.**

"Butter comes from cows. Tell me where the heck margarine comes from, and then maybe I'll eat it!"

–Phyllis, organist, 72

BRAN MUFFINS

1 (15-oz) box Raisin Bran
5 cups flour
1½ cups sugar
2 tsp salt
2 tbsp baking soda
3 tbsp cinnamon
2 tbsp nutmeg
Zest of one large orange
4 eggs, beaten

1 cup vegetable oil
1 qt buttermilk
½ cup raisins
½ cup dried cranberries or cherries
1 cup chopped dates
12 chopped prunes
12 chopped dried apricots
1 cup chopped walnuts

These bran muffins are delicious. The batter will keep for up to six weeks in the fridge, so you can make them in small batches as you want them.

Mix dry ingredients. In a separate bowl, mix wet ingredients. Blend the two together and then fold in dried fruit and nuts. Bake at 350°F for 20 minutes. **Makes 3 dozen, perfect for a brunch-time potluck.**

BROWN BETTY

2 tbsp butter	Grated rind and juice of
2 cups soft bread crumbs	1 fresh lemon
or finely chopped bread	$\frac{1}{4}$ tsp cinnamon
$\frac{1}{2}$ cup sugar	$\frac{1}{4}$ tsp nutmeg
	3 cups chopped apples

Be careful when making this recipe for your husband; he'll fall in love with Betty.

Melt butter and stir in crumbs. In a separate bowl, stir to combine the sugar, lemon rind (but not the juice), and spices. Pour enough buttered crumbs into a buttered dish to cover the bottom. Add half the apples. Sprinkle with half the sugar-spice mixture, then add more crumbs, the rest of the apples, and the rest of the sugar and spices. Top with the rest of the crumbs. Mix lemon juice with $\frac{1}{4}$ cup water and drizzle it over top.

Cover with aluminum foil and bake about 45 minutes in a 350°F oven. Remove the foil and put it back in the oven for a few minutes, until the top is brown and crispy. **Makes 6 to 8 helpings.**

Thrifty Brown Betty
Crushed cornflakes may be used instead of bread crumbs.

BRUNCH EGGS

12 eggs
4 cups milk
1 tsp salt

2 tsp dry mustard
8 slices of bread, cubed
1 lb Velveeta, cubed

A family favorite. Beat together the egg, milk, salt, and dried mustard. Place the cubed bread in a greased 9-by-13-inch pan. Cover with the egg mixture. Add cheese, pushing it down into the milk and bread mix. Let sit in fridge overnight. Bake for 1 hour at 350°F. **Makes about 8 helpings.**

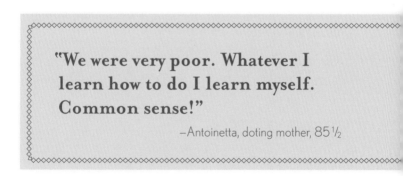

"We were very poor. Whatever I learn how to do I learn myself. Common sense!"

—Antoinetta, doting mother, 85½

BUTTERMILK BISCUITS

2 cups flour
1 tsp salt
2 tsp baking powder
½ tsp baking soda

1 tsp sugar
4 tbsp butter
½ cup buttermilk

For breakfast sandwiches or sopping up the sun-yellow yolk of a fried egg, nothing will treat you better than a buttermilk biscuit. These are also great served with gravy.

Combine the first 5 ingredients in a bowl and then cut in the butter until it is the size of small pebbles. Stir in buttermilk slowly. Knead dough a few times on a floured surface and use cookie cutter (or turn over a cup) to cut out circles. Bake for 10 to 12 minutes in a 450°F oven. **Makes about a dozen biscuits.**

COFFEE CAKE

2 cups flour
1 tsp baking soda
1 tsp baking powder
½ tsp salt
½ cup butter
1¼ cups sugar

2 eggs
1½ tsp vanilla
1 cup sour cream
Cinnamon-Sugar for
  topping (page 20)
½ cup chopped nuts

The perfect side dish for gossip, coffee cake should always be served when ladies come over for a midmorning coffee klatch.

Stir together flour, baking soda, baking powder, and salt. Mix up the butter and sugar and then crack in the eggs. Mix. Stir in vanilla and sour cream and then the flour mixture. Spread half the batter in your cake pan, sprinkle with a layer of cinnamon-sugar and nuts, add the rest of the batter and top with more cinnamon-sugar. Bake 50 minutes to 1 hour in a 350°F oven. Put on the kettle. **Makes 1 10-inch tube cake or 1 sheet cake.**

CINNAMON-SUGAR SPRINKLES

¼ cup sugar
1 tbsp cinnamon

Sugar and spice and everything nice: Keep a jar of cinnamon-sugar in your cupboard, and you'll always have a sweet homemade topping for buttered toast, coffee cake (page 18), or other treats.

Stir sugar and cinnamon until the color is mixed to a light brown. **Makes about ¼ cup.**

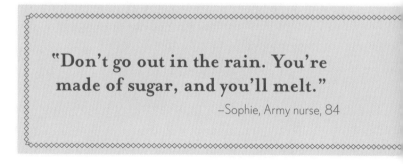

"Don't go out in the rain. You're made of sugar, and you'll melt."

–Sophie, Army nurse, 84

DOUGHNUTS

2 cups flour
½ cup sugar
½ tsp salt
4 tsp baking powder
½ tsp cinnamon

A little grated nutmeg
½ cup milk
2 tsp melted butter
1 egg, beaten
Hot fat for frying

Hot fat is a beautiful thing. Not beautiful like Robert Redford, but a more useful, Clint Eastwood–kind of beauty. The type of hot fat you choose is up to you: peanut oil, vegetable oil, shortening, and lard all work wonders.

Mix together flour, sugar, salt, baking powder, cinnamon, and nutmeg. Add milk and butter to the beaten egg, and whisk to combine everything. Knead lightly. On a well-floured board, roll dough about ¼-inch thick and cut with a doughnut cutter or upside-down cup. Roll scraps into small balls. Fry everything—scraps and all—in a pot of deep, hot fat. Fat should be hot enough to brown a cube of bread in 1 minute. If fat is too cool, doughnuts will absorb it. Once doughnuts are crispy and golden brown, drain them for a moment on paper towels, then move to a cooling rack. **Makes about 2 dozen donuts.**

EGGS IN A NEST

4 bread slices
Few pats of butter
4 eggs

Eggs and buttery toast taste even better combined. You might know this dish that nestles an egg inside toast as eggs in a hole, toast eggs, egg eyes, Devil's eyes, or God's eye bread.

Cut a circle from the center of each bread slice. Heat butter in a frying pan, add bread, and break an egg inside each hole. Cook until the bottom of the egg turns white and the bread is golden brown; then flip and cook the other side. The yolk should be runny.

Save the cutout bread circles and let them get nice and stale. Now you can use them for bread pudding (page 124). **Makes 4.**

"A grandmother isn't the same thing as a restaurant. Shut up and eat the eggs."

—Ruth, transcriptionist, 77

FROSTED CINNAMON ROLLS

1 packet yeast
1 tbsp sugar
3 cups flour
1/2 tsp salt
3/4 cup milk
1/4 cup brown sugar

1 tbsp cinnamon
3 1/2 tbsp melted butter, divided
1 cup powdered sugar, for frosting

Nothing screams weekend breakfast like screaming, "Weekend breakfast!" from your kitchen to wake everyone up when the cinnamon rolls are done. This tactic should be used only for naughty children or husbands who need to get work done; everyone else can sleep in and wake up naturally to the smell of these fresh buns.

Mix yeast and the 1 tbsp sugar with 1/4 cup of lukewarm water. In a separate bowl, mix flour and salt. After yeast has bubbled, mix in milk and 1 1/2 tbsp of the melted butter into it. Then combine it with the flour mixture. Knead until smooth, put in a greased bowl, cover with a damp tea towel, and let rise until doubled.

Mix brown sugar and cinnamon in a bowl. Punch dough down, and roll into a rectangle 1/4-inch thick. Brush with the remaining 2 tbsp melted butter, and sprinkle with the cinnamon-brown sugar combination. Roll up tightly and pinch the seam. Cut into rounds approximately 1 inch thick. Place on baking sheet and let rise for another 30 minutes. Bake in a 350°F oven for 20 to 30 minutes, or until buns start to turn golden.

To frost, mix teaspoons of water into a bowl of powdered sugar until it's smooth and creamy. Drizzle over hot rolls. **Makes a baker's dozen.**

GRITS

2 cups grits
Pinch of salt

Calling grits "porridge" or "gruel," as so many do, is a disgrace to this great corn cereal. We shouldn't act like we're all downtrodden Oliver Twists; and please, sir, we should all want more grits.

Soak grits in two quarts salted water overnight and then boil 45 minutes. Serve with milk and sugar or let them cool and cut into slices for frying alongside butter and bacon. **Makes enough for 4 to 8 helpings.**

OATMEAL

1 cup rolled oats
½ tsp salt

Oatmeal is as much about the oats as Vegas is about the desert—sure, you always see it there, but it's not the main attraction. It's *what* you stir into your oatmeal that counts, whereas in Vegas it's how many times you can visit the buffet and play penny slots before seeing Barry Manilow.

Bring 2 cups of water to a boil and stir in oats and salt. Reduce heat and cook until mushy, stirring occasionally. **Serves 2.**

Basic Oatmeal
Top with brown sugar and a bit of cream.

Apple Cinnamon Oatmeal
Stir in a chopped apple and 1 tsp cinnamon.

Prune Dee-lite Oatmeal
Add 1/2 cup of chopped prunes during last few minutes of cooking, allowing them to soften.

PANCAKES

1 cup flour	1 cup milk
2 tsp baking powder	1 tsp melted butter, plus a
¼ tsp salt	few pats for the skillet
1 egg	

Flapjacks, griddlecakes, whatever you call 'em, these golden-brown breakfast treats are best topped with a pat of sweet butter and pure maple syrup. In a pinch, Karo syrup costs pennies on the dollar, and it makes a fine pancake topper.

Mix flour, baking powder, and salt. Beat in egg. Stir in milk gradually to make a smooth batter and then add the melted butter. If batter's too thick, add a splash more milk. Mix in blueberries, sliced bananas, strawberries, or chocolate chips, if you like.

Heat a skillet and grease it with butter or a piece of bacon fat. Pour batter onto the skillet. When pancakes are full of bubbles, flip with a spatula and brown the other side. Serve in stacks with butter and warm maple syrup. **Serves 4 to 6.**

"I don't like to brag, but usually everything I make is good."

—Frances, office assistant, 87

PRUNE BREAD

$1\frac{1}{2}$ cups flour
1 tsp baking soda
$\frac{1}{2}$ tsp salt
$\frac{3}{4}$ cup sugar

2 eggs
1 tbsp butter
$\frac{1}{2}$ cup buttermilk
1 cup prunes, chopped

Keep yourself healthy with this prune-filled breakfast bread. If you really love your fiber, you can make half the flour whole-wheat, or replace some of it with wheat bran or germ.

Stir together flour, baking soda, salt, and sugar. Crack in the eggs. Add butter and buttermilk and stir in the prunes. Pour into loaf pan. Bake for about 45 minutes in a 325°F oven. Cut prune loaf into thick slices and slather on lots of butter or cream cheese. Makes 1 loaf.

"Stop it with your 'regular' jokes. Prunes are delicious. You wouldn't talk poorly about dried plums, right? Trick question!"

—Jeanette, rose enthusiast, 73

PUMPKIN BUTTER

3 or 4 pumpkins
About 1 tbsp cinnamon

Like good-looking people, pretty pumpkins are often really stupid on the inside. Find an ugly, knobby variety for this recipe, because it's likely to be sweeter. Also keep this point in mind when looking for a husband.

Peel and cut enough pumpkin to fill a large pot. Add a little water if it's dry and stew it for 4 or 5 hours, until it's a rich golden-brown color and has dried to a thick paste. Stir now and then to keep it from burning. Mash and add cinnamon or whatever spices you have on hand. Can or store in the fridge. Try pumpkin butter on toast or as a surprise layer between cakes. **Makes enough to eat on toast for several weeks in a row.**

REFRIGERATOR JAM

3 cups strawberries,
 raspberries, or mixed
 berries
2 cups sugar

You don't have to go to a lot of trouble and get out all your canning supplies to make jam. This easy recipe makes a small batch that will keep in the fridge for a few weeks.

Cut tops off berries, mash, and cook quickly on the stove until mushy. Mix in sugar and let sit for several hours.

Put the sugared fruit into a pot and cook gently until clear and thick. Spoon it into small jars and refrigerate. **Makes a few jars, give or take.**

"Don't work too hard."

–Nancy, mural-tour maven, 69

IRISH SODA BREAD

2 ¼ cups flour
1 tbsp baking soda
2 eggs

1 cup buttermilk
2 cups raisins, plumped in
  water and drained

Real Irish soda bread is simple, like this—don't let anybody serve you some fancy two-bit fruitcake and tell you it's the real thing. Irish eyes won't be smiling.

Mix ingredients in turn. Add raisins. Briefly knead dough on a floured surface. Place into buttered and floured 8-inch round pan. Dough will be sticky. Bake approximately 45 minutes in a 350°F oven. **Makes 1 loaf.**

USTIPKE

2 cups flour	4 eggs
Pinch of salt	1 cup milk
Pinch of sugar	Oil for frying

These Yugoslavian bits of fried dough make a fine and filling breakfast or snack served with cream cheese and jam.

Blend together all ingredients. Drop by wooden spoonfuls into hot oil and cook until golden brown on one side; flip and brown on the other side. Drain on paper towels. **Serves 4 to 6.**

"Crocheted blankets are uglier than knitted ones."

—Grace, gas station owner, 77

SOUPS, SALADS, *and* CASSEROLES

So much attention goes to dinner, but a casual luncheon or a potluck supper is often the most enjoyable of meals. When attending any such gathering, it's always in good form to ask the hostess what you should bring. Even if she says not to worry about it, a small gift that she can save for later—such as a jar of preserves or a houseplant—is always welcome, unless she explicitly states "no gifts." That's when you should ask yourself: Do I really want to be visiting the home of a woman who doesn't like gifts?

SOUP STOCK

Shin of beef or other discarded beef meat and bones, or the leftovers of a carved turkey or chicken 1 onion	2 celery stalks A combination of carrots, carrot tops, potatoes, turnips, or other vegetables

Fresh foods give the best flavors, but stock isn't the place for freshness; it's a catchall for leftovers. A woman who throws out old chicken bones, wilting carrot tops, and leftover beef might as well line her trashcan with money and call herself Mrs. Wastealots Rockefeller.

Put all the ingredients into a large pot with cold water, using about a quart of water per pound of meat, bone, and vegetables. Cover and simmer for several hours. Strain to separate the liquid stock from the meat and veggies and skim the fat off the top of meaty stocks before using. **Make stock in big batches and freeze until you're ready to use it.**

"Cheap food will taste expensive if you know what to do with it."

–Mary, housewife, 72

BORSCHT

3 red beets, peeled
1 onion
Half a green cabbage
3 tbsp butter

1 qt vegetable, beef, or
 chicken stock
Sour cream, to serve

This bright soup is a joy to eat and can be served hot or cold. Served cold, it is a most refreshing dish on a hot day. Be careful to always wear an apron while cooking it; beet stains are difficult to remove.

Mince the beets, onion, and cabbage; put in a pot with the butter and cook until vegetables start to soften. Add the stock; cover and simmer for an hour. Season with salt and pepper and serve with a dollop of sour cream on top. **Makes 4 to 8 helpings, depending on how much you like beets.**

"Be happy? I'm too old to be happy."

—Dobrila, cook, 70

CHICKEN NOODLE SOUP

4 quarts chicken broth
1 onion, chopped
2 cloves garlic, minced
3 stalks celery, chopped
4 carrots, sliced
1 tsp basil (or try thyme, rosemary or tarragon)

3 cups cut-up cooked chicken
1 package egg noodles
¼ cup chopped parsley
Plenty of salt and pepper

Flu shots are for people with a general lack of gumption and bad chicken soup recipes. This hearty, brothy soup serves as the cure for many ills and ailments, especially when punched up with matzoth balls (page 115).

Bring the broth to a boil in a large pot. Add onion, garlic, celery, carrots, and herbs. Reduce to a simmer and cover for about 10 minutes. Return soup to a boil and add chicken, noodles, and parsley. Reduce to a simmer and cover until noodles are cooked. Add salt and pepper to taste. Makes enough to feed all the sick ones home from work and school.

CHILI CON CARNE

1 lb beef, cut in small
  pieces or ground
2 tsp fat
1 tsp chili powder
1 onion, chopped
½ cup chopped tomato

1 small can tomato paste
½ tsp paprika
Pinch of salt
About 1 cup kidney beans
A few spoonfuls of flour

This is a great meal for the family, but never, ever serve a one-pot dish to dinner guests: It reeks of laziness and is the mark of a bad hostess. Complete the meal with a good corn bread (page 109).

Brown the meat in the hot fat, add chili powder and onion, and cook a few minutes more. Add the chopped tomato, tomato paste, paprika, salt, and a cup of water and cook until the meat is tender. Drain beans and add to the meat. Bring to a boil and thicken with a couple spoonfuls flour if necessary. Serve hot. Serves a family of 4 for dinner, likely with leftovers to freeze.

"I didn't eat. I drank coffee and I smoked cigarettes."

—Sylvia, mother of eight, 92

CORN CHOWDER

2 onions, sliced
3 tbsp butter or fat
2 tbsp flour
4 potatoes, sliced

1 can or 2 cups fresh corn, cooked
3 cups scalded milk
Salt and pepper

Equally a pleasure in summer and winter, corn chowder is such an easy dish. After you've made it a few times, you won't even need to look at a recipe. Just add the general amounts and work off taste.

Fry onion in fat and add flour, stirring so often that onion doesn't burn. Add 2 cups water and the potatoes; cook until the potatoes are soft. Add corn and milk and cook 5 minutes. Season and serve. Great with seafood. **Makes 1 big pot.**

"If you get a run in your stocking, use the part that's still good to keep onions. Put an onion in, knot it up, put another one in, and so on. Cut them off one by one when you need them."

–Juliette, bargain hunter, 83

SPLIT PEA SOUP

Ham bone	Package of green split peas
½ cup onion, chopped	Salt and pepper
2 stalks celery, chopped	1 carrot, sliced

A hearty dish, this soup can be served as an appetizer or a main dish with bread.

Add first 5 ingredients to a large pot of cold water. Bring to a boil and then cover and simmer for about 3 hours, stirring occasionally. About 20 minutes before serving, remove the ham bone and stir in sliced carrot. Makes enough for dinner and a week's worth of leftovers. Freeze and serve when you don't know what to make for dinner.

"Always wear clean underwear, in case you are in a car accident."

—Mary, housewife, 72

DANDELION SALAD

4 cups dandelion greens
(may substitute endive or
romaine)
3 slices bacon
1½ tbsp flour
1 egg

¼ cup vinegar
2 cups milk or water
1 tsp salt
2 tbsp sugar
3 hard-boiled eggs, sliced

Wash greens. Cut bacon into small pieces and fry until crisp; remove from drippings. Mix flour and 1 1/2 tbsp water in a bowl, then stir into pan with bacon drippings on medium heat. Mix egg, vinegar, and milk in a bowl, then slowly stir into pan mixture until well blended. Stir in salt and sugar. Cook until thickened; cool slightly. Pour over dandelion greens and garnish with sliced eggs and crisp bacon. **Serves 4.**

"My mother never knew what she was doing; she just did."

–Gloria, stenographer, 79

COLESLAW

1 cabbage	1½ tsp mustard powder
1 green pepper	½ cup mayonnaise
3 big carrots	¼ cup sour cream
1 onion	3 or 4 tbsp vinegar
2 tbsp sugar	

The ultimate barbecue picnic dish, coleslaw is crunchy, sweet, and tangy. Serve it as a side, pair it with baked beans, or even slap it on top of your burger. Just don't leave anything with mayo in the sun too long, unless you're serving it to someone you hate.

Grate vegetables together. Combine sugar, mustard powder, mayo, sour cream, and vinegar separately and then mix into the slaw. Let stand in the refrigerator a few hours before serving. **Makes 10 helpings.**

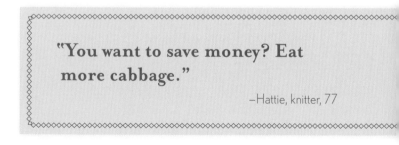

"You want to save money? Eat more cabbage."

–Hattie, knitter, 77

AMBROSIA

1 pineapple
2 oranges
1 grapefruit

1 cup sugar
Juice of 1 lemon
½ cup grated coconut

Did you know *ambrosia* means "food of the gods"? What a silly name for a fruit salad. I mean, it's good, but have the gods never tried lobster? Serve this delight at buffet-style meals where people can choose to eat it as either a side dish or a light dessert.

Cut the pineapple into 1-inch slices, then pare and twist off pieces with a strong fork. Pare the oranges and grapefruit and separate into sections, removing membrane between. Sprinkle with 1 cup sugar and lemon juice. Chill in icebox several hours. When ready to serve, mix with the coconut. **Makes 10 to 15 servings.**

JELLIED WALDORF SALAD

1 cup diced apples
1/4 cup diced celery
1/4 cup chopped figs
2 tbsp mayonnaise
2 tbsp sugar
1/3 cup lemon juice

1/4 tsp salt
2 tbsp gelatin
2 red pimientos, cut in
  small strips
Lettuce

Light, crisp, and refreshing, this molded salad makes for a dramatic presentation.

Mix fruits with mayonnaise, sugar, lemon juice, and salt. Soften gelatin with 1/4 cup cold water, then dissolve with 1 1/2 cups boiling water. Stir salad into the gelatin and pour into mold. When congealed, serve with mayonnaise and a pimiento garnish on top of lettuce leaves. **Serves 12.**

LAYERED LETTUCE SALAD

1 small head lettuce
1 cup diced celery
1 onion, diced
4 hard-boiled eggs, diced
1/2 cup green pepper, diced
1/2 cup red pepper, diced
1 (10-oz) package frozen
peas (do not thaw)
3/4 cup mayonnaise
1/4 cup sour cream
2 tbsp sugar
10 slices bacon
4 oz or more grated
cheddar cheese

Layer lettuce, celery, onion, eggs, peppers, peas. Mix mayonnaise,
sour cream, and sugar and pour over top of salad. Fry bacon until
crisp; break it into crumbles. Sprinkle bacon and cheese on top.
Cover and refrigerate. **Serves 4 to 6.**

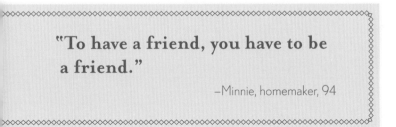

"To have a friend, you have to be
a friend."

–Minnie, homemaker, 94

MACARONI SALAD

3 hard-boiled eggs	2 onions
2 green peppers	Mayonnaise
1 or 2 pimientos	4 cups boiled macaroni

Delicious and easy to make, this salad is a picnic staple. Add more or less of any ingredients to taste.

Chop the first 4 ingredients finely, mix with mayonnaise, and pour over macaroni. Stir. Provides several potluck-sized servings.

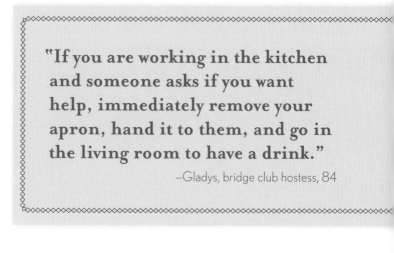

"If you are working in the kitchen and someone asks if you want help, immediately remove your apron, hand it to them, and go in the living room to have a drink."

–Gladys, bridge club hostess, 84

POTATO SALAD

6 cold, boiled potatoes
2 hard-boiled eggs
½ onion, grated
1 tsp dry mustard
Pinch of salt

Speck of pepper
2 tbsp vinegar
1 cup milk or cream
1 tbsp butter

Potato salad is a good medium for those who like customizing their foods. Delicious in its basic state, it takes additions like herbs and spices well. Try adding oregano and thyme, pimiento and sardines, or a bit of turmeric and hot sauce.

Cut potatoes in small cubes and add chopped egg whites and onion. Mash egg yolks with mustard, salt, and pepper. Mix together thoroughly and add vinegar. Bring milk or cream to boil and pour slowly over egg mixture, then add butter and pour over the potato mixture. Stir. Cool and serve on lettuce with a little more boiled dressing. **Makes 1 big bowl, about 12 helpings.**

SWEET POTATOES
with MARSHMALLOWS

5 or 6 sweet potatoes or yams	1 tsp salt
½ cup brown sugar	Juice of ½ orange
3 to 4 tbsp butter	½ tsp cinnamon
	2 cups mini marshmallows

Show me a Thanksgiving without marshmallow-topped sweet potatoes, and I'll show you one annoyed lady. Though you'll normally see these orange-and-white sweets around November, try 'em in the cold depths of February, when you need a little non-holiday pick-me-up.

Peel, cube, and then boil the sweet potatoes until tender—or used canned sweet potatoes. Mash. Then add sugar, butter, salt, orange juice, and cinnamon. Scoop into a greased casserole dish. Sprinkle the marshmallows on top and bake in a 350°F oven until the marshmallows look toasty. Serve hot. **Makes 6 to 8 servings.**

"If you can't think of anything nice to say, say it under your breath."

—Dorothy, bridge player, 82

GREATEST GREEN BEAN CASSEROLE

4 cups frozen green beans (the skinny ones), thawed	1¾ cups fried onions
Can of cream of mushroom soup	¼ cup milk
	¼ cup grated Parmesan
	Ground pepper

The secret to this version of the Thanksgiving classic is the same as the secret to many foods: Add some cheese.

Mix the green beans, soup, 1 cup of the fried onions, milk, Parmesan, and a little bit of pepper in a bowl. Scoop into a casserole dish and bake for 25 to 30 minutes at 350°F, or until the casserole is set. Top with remaining fried onions. Serves 6. If all the kids are in town for Thanksgiving, double or triple the recipe.

MACARONI *and*
CHEESE CASSEROLE

2 tbsp flour
1 tsp salt
$\frac{1}{2}$ tsp dry mustard
$\frac{1}{4}$ tsp pepper
$1\frac{1}{2}$ cups milk
2 tbsp butter
1 cup sour cream or plain
  yogurt

2 cups cheddar cheese
8 oz elbow macaroni,
  cooked 7 minutes and
  drained
$\frac{1}{2}$ cup breadcrumbs
  (optional)

I will admit, Kraft's blue box can be useful in a pinch, such as when a finicky 2-year-old guest refuses to eat real food. But if you want the best noodle-and-cheese experience, you have to bake it.

Combine the first 4 ingredients in a saucepan; stir in milk. Add butter, stirring constantly, and bring to a boil for 1 minute. Remove from heat and stir in sour cream or yogurt.

Stir in cheese and elbows. Pour into greased casserole dish and top with breadcrumbs if using. Bake at 375°F for 25 minutes, or until crunchy and golden brown on top. Makes 1 cheesy casserole.

Sissy Version
Replace whole milk with skim milk and regular macaroni with whole-wheat macaroni. Enjoy it less.

TUNA SURPRISE CASSEROLE

3 cans tuna
1 package frozen peas

1 can cream of mushroom
  soup
1 bag potato chips

Tuna surprise isn't just a casserole—it's a lifesaver for busy women. If the afternoon meeting of the women's auxiliary runs late, there's still time to run home, throw these pantry ingredients together, and have a satisfying dinner ready for your family in 30 minutes.

In a casserole dish, layer ingredients, starting with the tuna and ending with a thick layer of potato chips for a nice crunchy topping. Bake 25 minutes in a 350°F oven. **Serves 4.**

TURNIP CASSEROLE

| 2 lb purple-top turnips | 2 cans cream of celery soup |
| 10 oz good cheddar cheese | ½ bag herb-seasoned stuffing mix |

Small turnips are mild; big ones are stronger. It's your choice.

Peel turnips and boil until just done. Slice. Grate cheese coarsely. Mix the celery soup with ½ cup water. Layer all the ingredients in a casserole dish, starting with half the dry stuffing mix and ending with the other half of the stuffing mix and cheese on top. Bake until browned and bubbly, about an hour at 350°F. Serves 4 to 6.

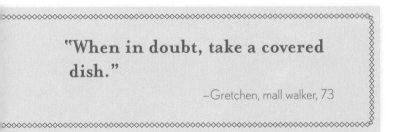

"When in doubt, take a covered dish."

–Gretchen, mall walker, 73

APPETIZERS *and* REFRESHMENTS

Being a good hostess is like winning a war: you don't react, you make preemptive strikes. Prepare as much as possible before your guests arrive, so they aren't chatting among themselves while you buzz about the kitchen, frantically making excuses like Nixon trying to talk his way out of Watergate. Remember that when you're hosting any event, food and drink are an excuse for socializing, not the other way around. Hors d'oeuvres or snacks should be offered during cocktail hour, but not so much that appetites are spoiled.

CANDIED NUTS

2 egg whites
$\frac{1}{2}$ cup sugar
$\frac{1}{2}$ cup brown sugar
$\frac{3}{4}$ tsp cinnamon

$\frac{1}{2}$ tsp salt
2 cups pecan halves or
 other nuts

A good hostess makes big show-stopping meals, but a great hostess pays attention to the details. Place a bowl of these nuts in every room guests occupy during the cocktail hour before a dinner party; it'll give them something to munch on and help ensure people don't get sauced too quickly.

Whisk egg whites with a spoonful of water. Combine everything else but the nuts in another bowl. Coat the nuts in egg whites. Toss in sugar mixture. Spread on a greased baking sheet and bake 45 minutes at 250°F, stirring occasionally. **Makes about 2 cups. Do a double batch for parties.**

CHEESE DREAMS

½ lb cheddar cheese
1 egg
½ onion

Several slices of bread
3 strips raw bacon

Your guests will swoon over these oh-so-simple bites that combine three of the best things in the world: cheese, bread, and bacon. Now if only I could add a dash of Robert Redford in there, they'd be perfect.

Grate cheese into a bowl. Stir in egg and onion. Cut bread into little triangles and spread with the cheesy mix. Chop raw bacon and arrange it on top. Sprinkle with paprika for color. Broil for a few minutes just before serving. **Serves a party of 5 to 8.**

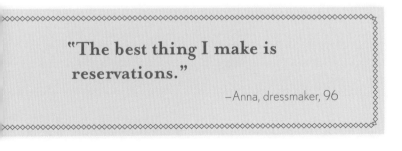

"The best thing I make is reservations."

–Anna, dressmaker, 96

DRIED BEEF *and* CHEESE BALLS

2 (8-oz) packages of cream cheese

6 green onions, tops included, chopped

1 tsp Worcestershire sauce

2 packages (5–6 oz) dried beef, chopped into little bits

A party isn't a party without a dip.

Mix all the ingredients except ¼ cup of the dried beef. Form into 2 small balls or 1 large one. Roll in remaining dried beef. Freezes well. Serves several with crackers at a party, and makes a great hostess gift.

DEVILED EGGS

4 hard-boiled eggs
¼ tsp salt
½ tsp dry mustard

¼ tsp cayenne
1 tsp vinegar
1 tbsp melted butter

If you plan to bring deviled eggs to a potluck, always check with the hostess first. They're a party staple, which means that someone should bring them, but not everyone. If that happens, not only will the only thing to eat be eggs, but the hostess's house will develop that pervasive egg smell.

When eggs are cold, remove shells and cut each in half lengthwise. Remove yolks and set whites aside. Rub yolks smooth and mix thoroughly with the rest of the ingredients. Roll into balls the size of the original yolk. Fill the hollow left in each eggwhite half with a ball of yolk mixture. **Makes 8.**

Fancy Deviled Eggs
When mixing yolks, add 4 boned anchovies, pounded smooth and strained. Or add ¼ cup chopped shrimp, chicken, or ham.

PIGS IN A BLANKET

| 1 package frozen puff pastry dough | 2 cans cocktail wieners or 1 package mini sausages |

Make this delicious and quick hot dish for when unexpected company comes around or when you're due at a potluck and discover the cheese you were going to use for the dried beef cheese ball has gone bad.

Wrap each wiener in a triangle of puff pastry, then place on a greased baking sheet. Bake in a 375°F oven until they are golden brown and puffy. Stick toothpicks in every pig for easy eating. **Serves a cocktail party.**

REFRIGERATOR PICKLES

2 tbsp kosher salt
1 cup vinegar
2 lb cucumbers (the
  littler ones)

4 cloves of garlic
Handful of fresh dill

People usually associate pickles with cucumbers, but with this recipe the cukes can easily be exchanged for carrots, green beans, beets, or even peeled watermelon rinds. If you like some heat, add a pinch of crushed hot pepper. Bay leaves, celery seeds, cloves, and whole peppercorns are also tasty pickling spices.

In a large pot, bring 2 cups water, salt, and vinegar to a boil and let it simmer. While that's happening, cut up your cucumbers to whatever size you like your pickles. Place them in a large bowl, add the garlic and dill, and pour the vinegar over everything. Cool to room temperature and let them refrigerate for at least a night before digging in. Makes about 2 lbs of pickles, because you put 2 lbs of cucumbers in. Nobody does math anymore.

SURPRISE BALLS

Mashed potatoes (page 116)
Leftover cooked meat,
  chopped up

Salt and pepper
A few pats of butter

This delicious snack turns leftover meat and mashed potatoes into an appetizer that everyone will love. Roll mashed potatoes into balls and then hollow the tops with a spoon. Stir a pinch of salt and pepper into the meat. Fill the crater in each ball with meat and smooth the potatoes around it. Place in a greased pan with a bit of butter on top of each ball. Brown in the oven and serve hot. If you've got lots of leftover meat and potatoes, make tons of surprise balls. These things go fast at parties!

"Don't wrinkle your forehead;
you'll get lines in your face."

–Rachel, ice-cream maker, 81

TURNOVERS

5 tbsp flour	2 cups ground cooked
$\frac{1}{2}$ tsp salt	meat
$\frac{1}{2}$ tsp paprika	Piecrust from page 146,
1 cup milk	made without sugar

These marvelous little savory pastries are great pick-up-and-eat food. They're also versatile and can be dressed up or down with the sauce of your choice.

Mix the dry ingredients in a saucepan. Place over medium heat and add the milk, little by little, until creamy. Add the meat. Set aside.

Roll the dough out and cut into 6-inch squares. Put a large spoonful of filling in the middle of each, wet the edges of the dough, fold it over, and use a fork to press down firmly. Make a small slit for air to escape. Bake for 15 to 30 minutes at 400°F. Makes 8, but you can make these smaller or larger, depending on how many people you'd like to serve.

CUCUMBER TEA SANDWICHES

1 cucumber
A few splashes of vinegar
About 8 slices of bread

Butter
Salt and pepper

Seed and slice the cucumber. Let it soak in vinegar for half an hour while you paint your toenails or pop over to the neighbor's. Drain. Butter bread, layer cucumber slices on top, and add a dash of salt and pepper. Cut off crusts and slice each sandwich into quarters. **Makes 16 sandwiches.**

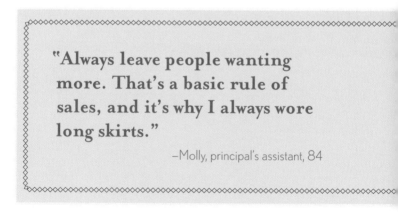

"Always leave people wanting more. That's a basic rule of sales, and it's why I always wore long skirts."

–Molly, principal's assistant, 84

TUNA SALAD SANDWICHES

1 can tuna	Salt and pepper
Mayonnaise	$\frac{1}{2}$ tsp mustard
1 stalk celery, chopped	Sliced white bread

Perfect for a casual lunchtime gathering, these sandwiches can be served halved as part of a buffet spread. Keeping the crusts on is optional.

Mix all ingredients and serve on white bread. Makes 2 sandwiches. Double or triple recipe as needed. Cut into quarters for a dainty teatime snack.

Egg Salad Sandwiches
Replace tuna with 2 chopped hard-boiled eggs.

TROPICAL BREEZE FRUIT LEATHER

2 cups mango chunks
2 bananas, broken into chunks
2 tbsp shredded coconut

Fruit leather is a delicious snack: it's like a fruit roll-up, except there's fruit in it. Heat oven to 140°F or its lowest setting and line a rimmed baking sheet with plastic wrap.

Blend all ingredients into a smooth fruit pulp. Pour onto the baking sheet and spread out mixture. Keep the thickness of the pulp at least 1/8 inch—it's OK if it doesn't reach the edges. The important thing is not to make the leather too thin or it will become brittle and crack, and you will feel like a terrible cook.

Put the fruit pulp in the oven and check periodically to see how it's cooking and to let any moisture escape. Depending on your oven and the thickness of the fruit, it will take between 3 and 10 hours to dry. Don't let it brown around the edges. Makes 2 to 6 servings, depending on how much you like the stuff.

GIMLETS

Gin
Half as much Rose's lime juice as gin
Lime wedges

Mix gin and lime juice in a shaker with ice. Shake till the outside gets frosty. Pour into cocktail glasses and garnish each with a lime wedge.

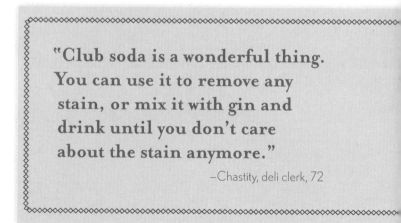

"Club soda is a wonderful thing. You can use it to remove any stain, or mix it with gin and drink until you don't care about the stain anymore."

—Chastity, deli clerk, 72

HOT TODDY

1 shot whiskey
6 cloves

1 tbsp honey
Juice of 1 lemon wedge

When winter colds attack, this boozy tonic is the cure. The sweet and boozy combination can help clear congestion, soothe a sore throat, and warm you up—all while making you care just a little bit less about being sick.

Pour whiskey, cloves, honey, and lemon juice into a mug. Top it off with boiling water and stir. Curl up with an afghan and a crossword puzzle or some reruns on TV. Makes 1.

LADIES' PARTY PUNCH

1 bottle cranberry juice
1 big can pineapple juice
1 bottle tea

½ bottle light rum
1 package frozen
   strawberries

Back before cosmos were the bees' knees, punch was what classy ladies drank. There was none of this "time to mix another cocktail" nonsense—you just gave yourself another ladle-full.

You'll want a fairly equal amount of cranberry juice, pineapple juice, and tea—adjust to your personal taste. In a punch bowl, combine all ingredients. Taste and then add more rum. Float partially defrosted strawberries in the punch. Enough for a party of 10.

"I call a handkerchief a crying towel, and I always keep one around when people are drinking. It's too easy to get sappy."

–Danielle, church choir soprano, 88

SUPPERS *and* SIDE DISHES

Gather the family, sit them at the table, and tell them they darn well better eat what you're serving. It's suppertime.

It's best to keep a sense of decorum at the dinner table; proper manners should be observed, and children should be encouraged to help by setting and clearing the table. There is a recent and shameful trend of families eating in front of the television. No matter how enjoyable *Wheel of Fortune* is, certain things, like Sundays and the music of Frank Sinatra, should remain sacred.

CHICKEN *and* DUMPLINGS

2 tbsp vegetable oil
1 onion, chopped
4 carrots, peeled and
  sliced
4 celery stalks
1 tsp dried thyme
3 qt chicken broth
1 tbsp hot sauce
Salt and pepper

1½ lb chicken, bones and
  skin removed
2 cups flour
2 tsp baking powder
1 tsp baking soda
1 tsp salt
1 tsp sugar
1 egg
1¼ cups milk

When your budget is tighter than a bad facelift, you can make a delicious dinner on little means by serving up a big pot of chicken and dumplings.

Heat oil in a large pot over medium-high heat. Cook onion until translucent. Add carrot, celery, thyme, and broth. Boil and then add hot sauce, salt, pepper, and chicken. Simmer until chicken is cooked, about 15 minutes. While chicken cooks, whisk together everything else.

When chicken is cooked, scoop it out of the pot and let cool. Keep stock simmering. Shred cooled chicken and return to stockpot. Bring to a boil and add dumpling batter in big spoonfuls. Simmer, covered, 10 minutes. Serve immediately. **Makes good dinner for 6, or 4 if you have big eaters.**

CHICKEN
DINNER *for* TWO

1 whole or 2 split chicken breasts	Salt and pepper to taste
2 large yams	1 tsp dried rosemary
Oil	1 or 2 cloves of crushed fresh garlic

Coat a frying pan with oil. Then place chicken, skin side down, in the middle of it. Cut yams with skin still on into quarters and place around chicken. Season your chicken and yams with salt, pepper, rosemary, and garlic. Place lid on pan and cook on medium heat. Cook for about 1 hour, or until fully cooked through. Turn chicken once during cooking to brown all sides. Place chicken and yams on platter, pour pan drippings on top, and serve.

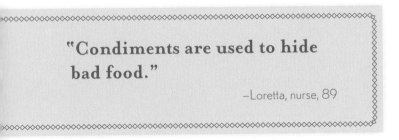

"Condiments are used to hide bad food."

–Loretta, nurse, 89

CHICKEN POTPIE

2 tbsp butter
2 tbsp flour
1/4 tsp salt
Dash of pepper
Dash of thyme
1/2 cup chicken broth
1/2 cup skim milk

2 cups cut-up chicken
2 diced carrots, steamed
1/4 lb green beans, in
  pieces, steamed
Piecrust from page 146,
  made without sugar

Show me a better dish for a cold winter's day than chicken pot-pie, and I'll show you a look of utter disbelief. Warm filling and flaky piecrust can chase even the deepest chills away.

Melt the butter in a saucepan and stir in the flour, salt, pepper, and thyme. Cook until thick. Add broth and milk until sauce is bubbling. Remove from heat, add chicken and vegetables, and stir.

Pour into a crust-lined pan, then top with the second crust and pinch the sides to seal. Cut a hole in the top and bake for 35 to 40 minutes in a 425°F oven. **Serves 6 to 8.**

FRIED CHICKEN

1 ½ lb chicken
Salt and pepper
2 pinches of ginger

Flour
¼ cup butter or poultry fat

Using a knife and fork or your fingers is equally fine for eating fried chicken, just be sure to keep lots of napkins close at hand. The last thing you want is to ruin a fine blouse with grease, especially at an event that eligible young men might be attending.

Season chicken with salt, pepper, and ginger. Dredge with flour and fry in plenty of hot fat in a frying pan until tender and brown, being careful not to burn. Serve right away or pack into picnic baskets along with lots of napkins. **Serves 4.**

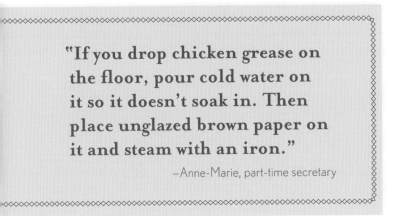

"If you drop chicken grease on the floor, pour cold water on it so it doesn't soak in. Then place unglazed brown paper on it and steam with an iron."

–Anne-Marie, part-time secretary

GOULASH

2 lb round steak
6 onions
2 pats butter
1 tbsp flour

1 tsp salt
1 tbsp paprika
2 cups sour cream
2 cups red wine

This Hungarian dish might look simple, but any family will love its flavorful meat.

Cut steak into strips. Brown onions and steak in butter. Add flour, salt, and paprika and let cook for a few minutes. Then mix it all up with the sour cream and wine. Pour into a casserole dish, cover, and bake for a little over an hour in a 375°F oven. Serves 5.

"We had to eat a lot of beans and greens, vegetables—that was during the depression. Mom made one thing, and you didn't get anything else. So you learned to like it."

–Rita, computer-card puncher, 80

LIVER *and* ONIONS

1 lb calf's liver, sliced
Salt and pepper
2 tbsp flour

2 tbsp goose or bacon fat
1 large onion, sliced

The modern aversion to this iron-rich dish is silly and quite a shame. Skin is an organ just like the liver, and people have no problem eating that.

Salt and pepper the liver to taste, then dredge with flour. Heat the fat in a frying pan. Fry the slices until brown on both sides. Push aside; add the onions and brown slightly. Cover and let cook 10 to 15 minutes.

Serve this dish with dumplings and a quick brown sauce: Take 2 tbsp butter, 2 tbsp flour, 1 cup stock of your choice (page 38), salt, and pepper. Brown the fat, add the flour and let brown, and then add the hot liquid and seasoning. Let cook 5 minutes, then pour on top of liver. **Makes a good family dinner.**

MEAT LOAF

1 or 2 eggs	1 tsp salt
1½ lbs ground beef or other meat	Onion and celery salt
¼ lb bread	½ cup canned tomato paste
¼ cup walnuts (optional)	A few strips of bacon

This dish turns you into a kitchen magician. By combining a few odds and ends, you can make ordinary meat extraordinary. Heck, if you can pull a rabbit out of a hat, feel free to grind it up and put it in there, too.

Beat an egg well and combine it with meat, bread, nuts, seasoning, and tomato. Mix thoroughly, form into a loaf, lay bacon strips on top, and place in roasting pan greased with a bit of fat. Bake in a 350°F oven for an hour, basting often. **Makes 1 loaf.**

Greet Loaf
Cut meat loaf in 1-inch squares and serve on crackers as an hors d'oeuvre at a party.

Loaf Around
Serve leftover meat loaf that is just "loafing around" on a sandwich with lettuce, tomato, onion, and mayonnaise.

Zeet Loaf
Serve a slice of meat loaf over ziti, covered with your favorite tomato sauce.

PORK CHOPS

4 to 6 pork chops
Salt and pepper

It's a sign of a good home if, even after a busy day, there are chops in the fridge for dinner.

Wipe chops, sprinkle with salt and pepper, place in a hot frying pan (with a little oil if they are very lean), and let them brown in their own fat for 2 to 3 minutes per side. Reduce heat, cover, and cook until chops are tender. Serve with applesauce or mint jelly. Serves 4 to 6. Cube leftover pork chops and bake them into a casserole.

Pork Chops Hawaiian

Marinate chops overnight before cooking in this mixture: 1 cup vinegar, 1/2 cup soy sauce, 1 cup brown sugar, 2 tbsp mustard powder, 6 cloves garlic (minced), 2 tbsp ginger (minced). Bake at 375°F for 40 minutes. Serve topped with pineapple rings sprinkled with brown sugar and sautéed in butter. Aloha!

POT ROAST

2 ½ lb beef (chuck, rump, or flank steak)
1 tbsp flour

2 tbsp drippings or oil
1 onion, chopped
1 or 2 bay leaves

There's nothing better than a good Sunday roast. Not only does the dramatic presentation make your family think you've made something extra-special for them, but you can use the rest of the roast for leftovers throughout the week, whether in sandwiches, chop suey, beef stew, or chili.

Season meat as desired and sprinkle with flour. Heat the fat and fry the onion in it until it's light brown; add the meat and brown on all sides to retain the juices. While meat is browning, boil 2 cups water. Pour it over the browned roast, add the bay leaves, and cover tightly. Simmer about 2 ½ hours, or until tender. Add a little boiling water to prevent burning, if necessary. Sliced or stewed tomato placed on top of the meat a half hour before serving makes a fine flavor. Thicken gravy with 1 tbsp flour. Makes a week's worth of good eats.

MEATBALLS

3 lb ground beef, veal, and pork
2 eggs, slightly beaten
1/2 cup grated Romano cheese

Salt and pepper to taste
2 cloves crushed garlic
Bread crumbs
Olive oil

To keep your meatballs as neat balls, don't make them too big—they're more likely to fall apart.

In a large bowl, mix the meats. Add eggs, cheese, salt, pepper, and garlic and just enough bread crumbs to hold the meat together when rolling into balls. Fry meatballs in some olive oil on low heat until browned on all sides. Save the oil from frying to add to the sauce (page 103). Makes plenty of meatballs for a big Sunday dinner. Serve over spaghetti with crusty bread to sop up the extra sauce.

SPAGHETTI SAUCE

1 can tomato paste
2 or 3 cloves garlic,
  chopped fine
2 tbsp olive oil

2 cans crushed tomatoes
1 can tomato puree
Meatballs (page 102)

Fry tomato paste and garlic in oil for a few minutes. Add all other ingredients, including the oil from frying the meatballs. Drop in meatballs and simmer for 3 to 4 hours. Season with salt and pepper, and add Italian seasonings to taste. With pasta, serves 4.

"The best meat has the blood
still in it."

–Gabriella, butcher's wife, 92

STUFFED CABBAGE ROLLS

1 head of green cabbage	½ tsp pepper
2 lb ground meat	3 lbs sauerkraut
1 cup long-grain rice	2 cups ketchup
1 tsp salt	2 cups white vinegar

Cabbage gets a lot of flack, but it's cheap and damn delicious. This recipe uses cabbage twice over, pairing the stuffed leaves with a heap of sauerkraut.

Core cabbage, place in boiling water, cover, and boil until leaves are pliable. Drain. Separate leaves and trim off thick outer veins. Combine meat, rice, salt, pepper, and mix well. Spoon mixture into center of cabbage leaves. Roll up and tuck in the ends. Line a big pot with a layer of sauerkraut. Place stuffed cabbage on top and keep layering with sauerkraut and stuffed cabbage until finished. Pour ketchup and white vinegar into the pot and add water until stuffed cabbage is completely covered. Cover and let cook until it bubbles on top. Reduce heat to a simmer and let cook for 6 hours. Makes 8 to 10 servings—good for a crowd.

BAKED BEANS
DELUXE

1 qt navy beans	2 tbsp molasses
½ lb salt pork	3 tbsp sugar
½ tbsp dry mustard	1 onion
1 tsp salt	

Baked beans are best served with brown bread; save your empty coffee cans to steam it in. Although thrift is always a virtue, do not skimp on the salt pork. It's what adds the majority of flavor.

Cover beans with cold water and soak overnight. Drain. Pour into a pot or casserole dish with the rest of the ingredients. Add enough water to cover the beans. Cover and bake in a 250° F oven for 8 hours. Serves 4 to 6, and tastes great with coleslaw.

"Use it up, wear it out, make it do, or do without."

–Thelma, homemaker, 88

BOSTON BROWN BREAD

1 egg
½ cup sugar
½ cup molasses
1 cup sour milk

2 tsp soda
1 tsp salt
2 ¾ cups graham flour

Between baked beans and this moist, molassesy bread, they're doing something right up in Boston.

Beat eggs, add sugar and molasses, and then the rest of the ingredients. Mix and place in 3 greased 1-pound coffee cans. Cover tightly. Steam 1 to 2 hours by placing on a steamer over boiling water, letting the water go about halfway up the can. Basically, you just don't want the can touching the bottom of the pot you're boiling in. (You can also steam the bread in a deep oven-safe pan in the oven itself. Just make sure to replenish the water if needed.) Bread is done when a toothpick comes out clean. **Makes enough to sop up lots of delicious baked bean juice.**

CORN BREAD

¼ tsp baking soda
1 ½ cups buttermilk
2 cups cornmeal

3 tbsp lard
1 tsp salt

A perfect accompaniment for chili and meat dishes, leftover corn bread is also excellent served with breakfast eggs.

Dissolve baking soda in buttermilk, add to cornmeal with lard and salt, and stir in about 1 cup water. Add more water if necessary. Bake in a greased 8-inch pan in a 350°F oven. Makes 6 to 10 squares.

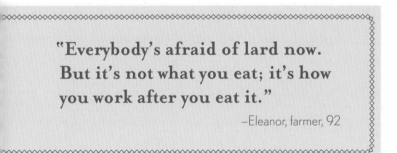

"Everybody's afraid of lard now. But it's not what you eat; it's how you work after you eat it."

–Eleanor, farmer, 92

GO-TO GREENS

1 peck greens of your choice
Salt pork

Greens should be tender and fresh. Wash them well, cutting off small roots. Put them into a big uncovered pot and fill it two-thirds with boiling water. Drain greens, add sliced salt pork, and cook in 1 qt boiling water for another 1 ½ hours, or until water evaporates. The time depends on how young and tender the greens are—taste them while they cook. If greens are still too bitter when done, cut the taste with a splash of cider vinegar. **Serves 4 to 6.**

"Smile pretty in case an available man is looking."

–Frieda, secretary, 87

HOT SLAW

1 lb double-thick bacon,
  cut into bite-size pieces
3 big yellow onions
½ lb carrots
About 1½ lb red cabbage

Scant ½ cup vinegar
1 tbsp caraway seeds

Say hello to coleslaw's daring cousin.

Fry bacon pieces, drain well, and push the bacon to the side of pan. Cut onions coarsely and sauté in the bacon pan. Cut carrots and add to pan. Cut cabbage in ribbons (as for slaw), add it to the pan, and cook briskly until it just starts to get soft. Add vinegar and caraway seeds, stir, and serve. **Makes 4 to 8 helpings.**

CREAMY BROCCOLI *and* ZUCCHINI

8 oz noodles
2 tbsp butter
½ cup grated parmesan cheese, plus more for topping
2 cups chopped fresh broccoli
2 cups chopped zucchini
½ cup chopped onion

1 clove garlic
1 lb sweet Italian sausage
3 tbsp flour
2 tbsp parsley
½ tsp salt
½ tsp dried oregano
¾ cup milk
1½ cups ricotta or cottage cheese

The name may make it sound like a side dish, but beefed (or, really, porked) up with sausage and noodles, this recipe makes an easy and filling weeknight dinner. You can replace the regular noodles with a spinach variety if you're thinking about your health.

Cook, drain, and butter noodles. Top with some grated Parmesan cheese. In a saucepan, cook broccoli and zucchini in small amount of boiling salted water until tender. Drain well. In large skillet cook onion, garlic, and sliced sausage until tender. Blend in flour, parsley, salt, and oregano. Add milk all at once. Cook and stir till bubbly. Add ricotta or cottage cheese. Cook and stir until cheese is nearly melted. Stir in the vegetables. Heat through and serve over hot cooked noodles. Pass more parmesan cheese around the table to sprinkle on top. Serves 4 to 6.

LATKES

2 potatoes, peeled and shredded	2 eggs
2 tsp baking powder	1 tbsp salt
	Oil, for frying

French fries, hash browns, or latkes: few people will complain when you bring fried potatoes to the table.

Squeeze water out of potatoes; add the baking powder, eggs, and salt. Form into pancakes and fry in oil. A good side dish or practically a meal unto themselves, these potato pancakes should be served with applesauce or sour cream. Makes 4 to 6 pancakes, depending on how large you like them.

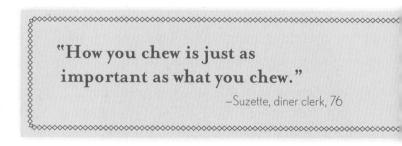

"How you chew is just as important as what you chew."

—Suzette, diner clerk, 76

MATZOTH BALLS

1½ sheets matzoth
2 cups matzoth meal
1 tbsp suet or other fat
1 chopped onion
3 beaten eggs

¼ tsp salt
⅛ tsp ginger
⅛ tsp mace
⅛ tsp pepper

Sure, you can make chicken noodle soup (page 42) without matzoth balls. You can also make a house with no roof. What's the point?

Bring a pot of salted water to a boil, then reduce it to a simmer. Soak the matzoth sheets in a little cold water and squeeze dry; add meal. Put suet in a frying pan, add onions, and cook until brown. Add matzoth mix, eggs, and seasonings and combine well. Form into balls and drop into the simmering pot. Cover and cook 30 to 35 minutes. Add to chicken noodle soup. **Makes 20 balls.**

{ MASHED POTATOES }

6 potatoes	**2 tbsp butter**
1 tsp salt	**1/3 cup hot milk**

You show me a better side dish than mashed potatoes, and I'll show you a unicorn. It doesn't exist!

Scrub, pare, and drop potatoes in cold water as they are pared to keep them white. If old or frozen, let stand in cold water half an hour. Place in boiling water and cook, covered, 20 or 30 minutes. When nearly done, add salt. Drain.

Rub potatoes through a ricer or mash and add the rest of the ingredients in order. Beat with a fork until creamy and pile lightly on a hot dish. Keep warm (as in a chafing dish over hot water) until ready to serve. Dot with butter and sprinkle with paprika. Serves 6.

PIEROGIES

2 eggs
3 cups flour
2 tsp salt, divided
1 lb lean raw beef
$\frac{1}{8}$ tsp pepper

$\frac{1}{2}$ tsp onion juice
1 onion, chopped
1 green pepper, chopped
Butter

You fry pierogies. You fry them with onions. I don't even know what to call it when people just boil them. Actually, I do know what to call it: a damn shame.

Beat the egg and then add the flour and 1 tsp of the salt. Add a splash of water if necessary. Knead and let stand for a half hour. This is a good time to hang the laundry on the line or straighten up the house.

Roll noodle dough into $1\frac{1}{2}$-inch square pieces. Mix the meat with the egg, seasonings, onion, and pepper, and place a teaspoon in each square. Fold into a triangle and press edges together. Drop in boiling water and cook for 15 minutes.

Fry pierogies in butter with onion and green pepper until they start to brown. Serves 2 to 4.

Potato Pierogies

Replace meat with mashed potatoes (page 116) mixed with some grated cheddar cheese.

{ **SWEETS** *and* **TREATS** }

A meal isn't over if it isn't finished with a bit of sugar. Calorie counting is the business of people who don't have their priorities straight; eating dessert is the business of people who love life.

Really, desserts are love in food form, and a well-baked dessert is a great way to show people how much you care.

BOURBON BALLS

1 cup toasted chopped pecans	3/4 cup powdered sugar
1 1/2 cups crushed vanilla wafer cookies	2 tbsp cocoa powder
	2 tbsp honey
	1/4 cup bourbon

The world is full of excuses; bourbon balls are an excuse to imbibe alcohol while eating candy. This is a good kind of excuse.

Combine first four ingredients in a bowl and then add honey and bourbon; stir. Form into balls with your hands and roll in powdered sugar. Refrigerate before serving. **Makes approximately 48 balls.**

"Don't wear dark lipstick. When it shows up on a man's collar, everyone is going to know it's yours."

–Elizabeth, teacher, 72

BREAD PUDDING

2 eggs
1 pint milk
½ cup sugar
Nutmeg or cinnamon
 (optional)

1 qt stale bread or cake
 cut into cubes
¼ cup seeded raisins
 (optional)
Almonds (optional)

Pigeons are filthy creatures and don't deserve to be fed. Save your stale bread for yourself, and make this delicious, custardy dessert.

Beat the eggs and then add milk, sugar, and gratings of nutmeg or cinnamon if desired; pour over the bread in a pudding dish, let stand until thoroughly soaked, and bake 30 to 40 minutes in a 350°F oven. Add seeded raisins and almonds if desired. **Makes about 12 helpings.**

"A little sugar never hurt anybody."

–Mary Louise, newspaper columnist, 91

FUDGE

2 cups sugar
2 tsp corn syrup
1 cup milk, cream, or
  water

4 tbsp cocoa
$\frac{1}{8}$ tsp salt
2 tbsp butter
1 tsp vanilla

Making friends is as easy as making fudge.

Cook sugar, syrup, milk, and chocolate over low heat. Stir occasionally to prevent burning and bring to a boil. Keep cooking until a bit of the mixture dropped into a glass of ice cold water forms a soft ball (234°F). Add salt, butter, and vanilla. Let cool until candy may be dented with a finger. Beat until thick and creamy. Pour in buttered pan. Mark in squares and let set. Makes 1 pan. A great gift boxed during the holidays.

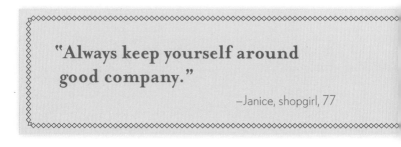

"Always keep yourself around good company."

—Janice, shopgirl, 77

GINGERBREAD

2 tsp baking soda
1 cup sour milk or
 buttermilk
1 cup molasses
1/2 cup butter
1 cup sugar
1 egg

3 cups flour
2 tsp ginger
1 tsp spices (cinnamon
 and clove)
1 qt blueberries
 (optional)

This isn't Christmas-house-making gingerbread, this is good ol' soft 'n' cakey gingerbread that's meant to be eaten in front of a fireplace, along with mulled wine.

Mix soda and sour milk and add to molasses. Cream butter, add sugar, then egg. Stir in flour and spices and berries rolled in some extra flour. Pour into a buttered 13-by-19-inch pan and bake 30 to 45 minutes in 350°F oven. Cover with whipped cream or frosting. Serves 15.

HOMEMADE ICE CREAM

7 eggs
1 cup sugar
1 can (about 13 oz)
 evaporated milk

2 tbsp vanilla
1 cup brown sugar
½ gallon milk

Why the heck would you freeze yogurt? This is the only summertime treat you need.

Beat eggs. Combine with all other ingredients. Pour into an ice cream freezer. Add rock salt and crushed ice to outside container. Crank until you can't crank anymore, about 30 to 45 minutes. Makes 5 quarts.

"Sometimes I feel sorry for myself, so I reward myself with candy or a piece of cake. Then I feel better."

–Hannah, gardener, 83

JELLYROLL

Jar of jelly or jam (pumpkin butter and frosting are also good)
3 eggs
1 cup sugar
Pinch of salt

1 tsp vanilla
$\frac{1}{2}$ cup warm milk with 1 tsp melted butter
1 cup flour
1 tsp baking powder

Be sure to wear sneakers when making this recipe, because you need to move fast.

Warm jelly or jam to make it easy to spread. Beat eggs and sugar and then add salt, vanilla, milk with butter, flour, and baking powder. Mix slowly and then pour into a greased jellyroll pan and bake in a 375°F oven for 13 minutes, or until a light golden brown.

When you take out the cake, scrape the edges of the pan with a knife and then invert the pan over a clean dishcloth; hopefully it will drop out. If it sticks, hit the back of the pan with a spoon. As soon as the cake is free, spread jam all over it. Then use the dish towel to roll it up very quickly. Keep the cake wrapped in the towel until it has cooled, then slice and serve. **Makes 12+ servings.**

APPLE MOLASSES BUNDT CAKE

1 cup butter	1 tsp nutmeg
3 cups sugar	2 tsp cinnamon
3 eggs	½ cup milk
1½ cups molasses	3 cups flour
2 tsp baking powder	2 to 3 apples
1 tsp cloves	

A fine treat for breakfast, afternoon tea, or after dinner when served with freshly whipped cream.

Cream butter and sugar; then add eggs, well beaten; then add molasses, spices, baking powder, and milk; then add flour and, lastly, apples peeled and cut in cubes. Bake in a greased Bundt pan in a 350°F oven for 35 or 40 minutes. Makes 1 cake.

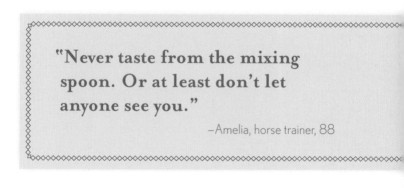

"Never taste from the mixing spoon. Or at least don't let anyone see you."

—Amelia, horse trainer, 88

REALLY GOOD CHOCOLATE CAKE

2 cups flour
2 cups sugar
½ cup plus 2 tbsp cocoa powder
1 tsp salt
2 tsp baking soda
1 tsp baking powder

1 cup vegetable or canola oil
1 cup milk
1 cup cold coffee
2 eggs
1 tsp vanilla

A perfect birthday cake, if you know anybody who's worth celebrating. Robert Redford's birthday is August 18.

Mix dry ingredients together in one bowl. Mix wet ingredients in another bowl. Then add the two together. Pour into two greased 8-inch round cake pans and bake 40 to 50 minutes (until a toothpick comes out clean) at 350°F. Cool on a wire rack. Makes 1 cake.

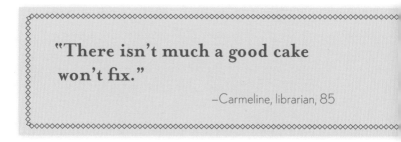

"There isn't much a good cake won't fix."

—Carmeline, librarian, 85

CHOCOLATE ICING

| 1 (12-oz) container of sour cream | 1 (10- to 12-oz) bag chocolate chips |

To really impress, don't tell people how simple this recipe is. You want them to think you're a great cook, not some Easy Emily.

Take sour cream out of fridge sometime before using. Half an hour is usually enough. Melt the chocolate chips in the microwave or in a small pot placed in a larger pot of water on the burner. Let chocolate cool about 10 minutes and then mix the two together, adding a little sour cream at a time. **Makes enough to frost one cake.**

JEWISH PEACH CAKE

3½ cups sugar, divided
1 tbsp cinnamon
3 cups flour
4 eggs
2½ tsp vanilla

3 tsp baking powder
1 cup oil
¼ cup canned peach juice
1 (1 lb, 13-oz) can peach
   slices, drained

Everyone will think you're a peach for serving this sunny cake.

Mix together and set aside ½ cup of the sugar and cinnamon. Stir together remaining sugar, flour, eggs, vanilla, baking powder, oil, and peach juice. Pour half the batter into greased tube pan. Layer half the peaches and sprinkle with half the sugar-cinnamon mixture. Repeat batter and peaches, ending with sugar mixture.

Bake in 350°F oven for 1 ½ hours. Remove cake from pan after letting cool no longer than 5 or 10 minutes. **Serves 10 to 12.**

POUND CAKE

1 pound cake flour
1 pound butter
1 pound sugar

1 pound eggs (about 9 or
 10 eggs)
2 tbsp vanilla or brandy

This is a cake that's earned its name.

Sift flour once. Cream butter well, add sugar gradually, and beat until light and fluffy. Add eggs, 2 at a time, and beat well after each addition; pour in vanilla or brandy. Slowly mix in flour and beat until smooth. Pour mixture into 3 (small) greased loaf pans and bake in a 300°F oven for about 1 hour and 15 minutes. Makes 3 cakes.

> "You're watching a cooking show? You're watching an idiot."
>
> —Hester, waitress, 73

CHOCOLATE CHIP COOKIES

1 ⅓ cups flour
½ tsp baking soda
½ tsp salt
½ cup softened butter
⅓ cup sugar

½ cup light brown sugar
1 egg
¾ tsp vanilla
1 cup chocolate chips

Everyone claims that their chocolate chip cookies are the best. Well, you know what? We aren't all bright and shining stars in the universe. These cookies are pretty darn good. That's all I'm going to say.

Mix flour, soda, and salt in a bowl. Cream together butter and sugars, then add egg and vanilla. Mix dry and wet ingredients together and then stir in chocolate chips. Drop small balls of dough onto a cookie sheet about 2 inches apart and bake about 8 to 10 minutes in a 350°F oven. **Makes about 2 dozen perfect cookies.**

OATMEAL RAISIN DROPPERS

2 sticks butter, softened
1 cup brown sugar
2 eggs
2 tsp vanilla
1 ½ cups flour
¾ tsp baking soda

½ tsp salt
Big pinch ground nutmeg
½ tsp cinnamon
3 cups rolled oats
1 ½ cups raisins

There's a place for ugly cookies. That place is the cookie jar, where they can break into pieces and it doesn't matter because they're still darn delicious.

Cream butter and sugar until fluffy. Mix in eggs and vanilla. Slowly beat in flour, baking soda, salt, nutmeg, and cinnamon. Stir in oats and raisins. Drop little balls of dough 2 inches apart on greased cookie sheets. Bake 12 minutes in a 350°F oven, or until brown on the edges but soft in the middle. Makes about 4 dozen, keeping your cookie jar filled for quite a while.

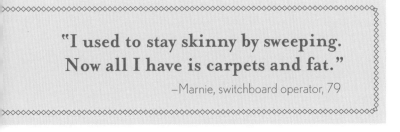

"I used to stay skinny by sweeping.
Now all I have is carpets and fat."

–Marnie, switchboard operator, 79

SUGAR COOKIES

1 ²/₃ cups flour
½ tsp baking powder
¼ tsp salt
Stick of butter, softened

¾ cup sugar
1 egg
1 tsp vanilla

Have the holidays really happened if you haven't frosted a sugar cookie? To be sure that you've celebrated, make these sweet treats.

Combine dry ingredients in a bowl. In a second bowl, blend butter and sugar and then add egg and vanilla. Combine the 2 mixtures, beating slowly. When dough is smooth, put in plastic and place in the fridge for a couple of hours.

Roll dough, cut out shapes, and bake for about 15 minutes at 325°F, or until edges are brown. When cool, decorate with Cookie Icing (page 144). These cookies are good to send to school with children because they hold up in lunchboxes. **Makes a big batch.**

COOKIE ICING

| 2 egg whites | 3 cups powdered sugar |
| 1 tbsp lemon juice | Food coloring |

Whisk all ingredients (except food coloring) together until thick. If icing seems too thin, add more powdered sugar. Divide into bowls and tint with food coloring. **Makes enough to frost a big batch of cookies.** Or sandwich it between graham crackers for a sweet afternoon snack.

ALL-PURPOSE VANILLA FROSTING

| 2 egg whites | 3 cups powdered sugar |
| 4 tbsp butter, softened | 1 tsp vanilla |

Turn any snack cake into an elegant dessert cake just by adding this frosting.

Beat the egg whites until thick and frothy. Add butter and sugar, a little at a time, until the frosting is thick (add more sugar if necessary). Beat in vanilla. If frosting starts to get mushy, stick it in the fridge for a little bit. **Makes enough to frost 1 cake or batch of cookies.**

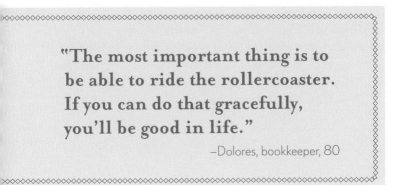

"The most important thing is to be able to ride the rollercoaster. If you can do that gracefully, you'll be good in life."

–Dolores, bookkeeper, 80

PIECRUST

4 cups flour	1 tsp sugar
Pinch of salt	1 ½ cups shortening
½ tsp baking powder	1 cup milk

In a large bowl, sift flour and add salt, baking powder, and sugar. Then add tablespoons of shortening to flour mixture, spreading it around and mixing it a little. With clean hands, slowly knead the shortening into the flour. It should stick together a little. Add milk slowly, mixing as you go, until most of it is incorporated. Then go back and knead it with your hands again. The final dough should stick to your hands, but you should still be able to work with it. Don't overknead! Let cool in a large plastic bag in the refrigerator for about 1 hour before using.

After the dough has chilled, dust your rolling pin and work surface with flour, then roll a circle as thin as you can so it covers the size of a pie plate. Place dough in plate and add filling. Add top crust if the recipe calls for it, and pinch edges of top and bottom crusts together. Make sure to cut slits in the top crust so steam can escape. **Makes enough crusts for 4 to 5 pies. Freeze dough you don't intend to use in the next few days.**

APPLE PIE

Piecrust (page 146)
4 to 6 apples
½ cup sugar

1 tbsp butter
Spices of your choice

Pare, core, and slice apples. Place in a bowl and mix with sugar, 1 to 2 tbsp water, bits of the butter, and your choice of spices (cinnamon, nutmeg, etc.). Pour into an uncooked piecrust and then lay the upper crust on top. Pinch edges, slash upper crust, and bake at 425°F for 35 to 45 minutes, or until the crust is golden brown on the edges. Makes 1 pie.

"Always keep a baking sheet on the oven's bottom rack when making pie to catch any filling that bubbles over. You don't want to scrub that thing."

–Meredith, poodle enthusiast, 95

RHUBARB PIE

3 cups fresh rhubarb
2 tbsp cornstarch
1½ cups sugar

1 egg, lightly beaten
Piecrust (page 146)

Chop rhubarb into bite-size pieces, then sprinkle with cornstarch. Toss it with sugar and egg. Spread into a piecrust. Bake in a 375°F oven for about 45 minutes. Keep your eye on it to prevent burning. **Makes 1 pie.**

Strawberry Rhubarb Pie
Replace half the rhubarb with freshly sliced strawberries.

PECAN PIE

1 tsp vanilla
1 cup pecans
1 cup white corn syrup
²/₃ cup sugar
Pinch of salt

¼ cup milk
5 tbsp butter
3 eggs
Piecrust (page 146)

Mix all ingredients together in a bowl. Pour into an uncooked piecrust. Bake at 250°F for 15 minutes and then 350°F for another 30 to 40 minutes, or until filling is firm. Makes 1 pie that will put all the other pies at the bake sale to shame.

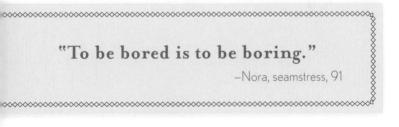

"To be bored is to be boring."

–Nora, seamstress, 91

PUMPKIN PIE

Piecrust (page 146)
1 cup pumpkin puree
1/4 cup sugar
1/2 tsp salt
1/4 tsp cinnamon

1/8 tsp mace
1/2 tsp vanilla
1 egg and 1 yolk
1/2 cup milk
1/2 cup cream

Everyone at Thanksgiving dinner will be thanking you for making this pie.

Bake crust in a 350°F oven for 15 minutes. While it's baking, mix all the filling ingredients and then pour into prepared crust. Cook for about an hour more, or until the pie is set. **Makes 1 pie.**

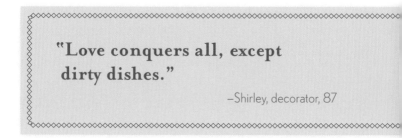

"Love conquers all, except dirty dishes."

–Shirley, decorator, 87

LEMON
MERINGUE PIE

Piecrust from page 146, baked at 375°F until it starts to brown at the edges

5 yolks

1 cup sugar

Juice and zested rind of two large lemons

5 egg whites

Powdered sugar

Beat yolks until light, then add sugar, lemon juice, and rind. Place in a double boiler (or fill a pot with water and put a smaller pot or metal bowl inside it). Cook until thick and smooth, stirring constantly. Let cool. While the yolk mix is cooling, beat the egg whites until stiff. Fold ¾ of the whites into the yolks. Place in crust. Add a bit of powdered sugar to the rest of the whites and beat a little more. Put sugary whites on top of the pie and place in a 350°F oven until peaks start to brown. Cool and then put in fridge to set. **Makes 1 pie.**

SELECTED BIBLIOGRAPHY

In addition to seeking out the wisdom of all the little old ladies in my neighborhood, I consulted the following books in compiling the classic, thrifty recipes included in this volume. These out-of-print volumes are rare gems you might find at a flea market or yard sale, if you're lucky! Many of them are available to read in full online.

The Atlanta Women's Club Cook Book
Castelar Creche Cook Book
King's Daughters Cook Book
Milwaukee Cook Book
Modern Women of America Cook Book
Mrs. Rorer's New Cook Book
The Settlement Cook Book
Victory Memorial Cook Book

INDEX *of* RECIPES

Meg Favreau is a writer, comedian, food enthusiast, and one-time eating-contest winner living in Los Angeles. Her work has appeared on sites including *the Huffington Post*, *McSweeney's*, and *the Smart Set*, and she serves as senior editor of the frugal-living and personal-finance site *Wise Bread*. Meg dedicates this book to her grandmother, whose pie-making skills remain unrivaled, and her mother, who once said, "I want the dedication in your first book to be 'To my mother, who always believed in me.'" (It's true.)

ABOUT *the* PHOTOGRAPHER

Michael E. Reali is a fervent photographer, intermittent painter, incidental mosaicist, desultory traveler, casual gourmand, and practiced chef who once spent a night trapped on a mountainside in Greece with a bull. A native of Philadelphia, his work can be seen on murals throughout the city as well as in the book *Old Man Drinks*, an assignment that landed him much acclaim and a stint at Betty Ford.

Mr. Reali possesses a degree in fine art as well as an extra bit of pancreas, making him a curiosity of modern medicine. All of Mr. Reali's proceeds from this book will go to his favorite charity: The Feed Mike Reali Fund.

{ ACKNOWLEDGMENTS }

Several people contributed their own recipes, as well as dishes from their mothers, grandmothers, and great-grandmothers. I am so very grateful, and without them this book would not exist. My deepest thanks to Dobrila Bokun, who fried up her Ustipke on a moment's notice; Bea Damiani, whose buttermilk and bran muffin batter just keeps giving; Norma Damiani, who understands the power of bacon in making greens edible; Beatrice Favreau, whose recipes live on as pretty much the only things my dad cooks other than plain rice; Suzanne Favreau, whose cooking made me love food; Robin Johnson, who has the perfect hot dish for any situation, from slaw to turnip casserole; Louise Kromko, the queen of stuffed cabbage; Anne O'Keefe, who understands that the best Irish soda bread is kept simple; Elizabeth Nestel, whose Jewish peach cake puts apple cake to shame; Florence Raffa, whose meatballs and sauce have fed Michael well over the years; Connie Riley, whose several recipes amount to a one-person potluck; Lucretia Sulimay, who successfully created her chocolate cake and frosting to be a more awesome version of the best boxed birthday cake; and Judy Taylor, whose dried-beef cheese ball brings party dip to a whole new (spherical) level.

I extend a hearty thank-you to the wonderful women who posed for the photographs in this book. Without them, it would be much less lively: Dobrila Bokun, Rita Brunelli, Thelma Calabrese, Pauline Capriotti, Eileen Carabello, Antoinetta Cutrufello, Bea Damiani, Norma Damiani, Nancy Davis, Santina DeAngelis, Maria DiMarcello, Emma Fala, Edith Greenspan, Lydia Hantman, Phyllis Herman, Alma Hill, Robin Johnson, Julia Kilgallen, Dorothy Kristman, Louise Kromko, Rose Marchese, Frances Marinaro, Charlotte McGinnis, Jean McParland, Mary Morrone, Kathleen Moss, Catherine Mowbray, Elizabeth Nestel, Anne O'Keefe, Mary Paoletti, Florence Raffa, Sylvia Richter, Connie Riley, Margaret Schafer, Margie Taggart, Judy Taylor, Dolores Welker, and Loretta White.

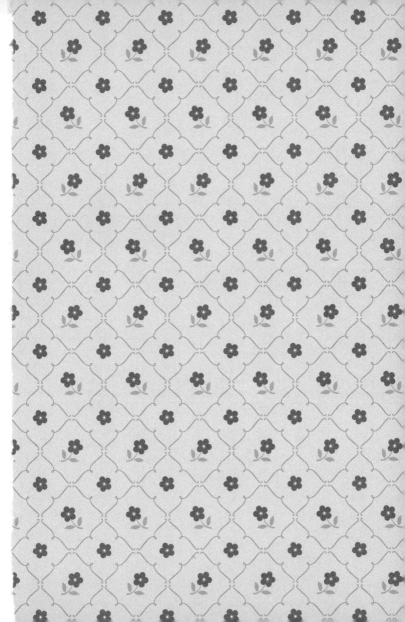